The Four Seasons!

By Ruth Thomson

Pictures by Catherine Bradbury

Gareth Stevens Publishing
Milwaukee

BRIGHT IDEA BOOKS:

First Words!
Picture Dictionary!
Opposites!
Sounds!

Mouse Count!
Time!
Animal 1*2*3!
Animal ABC!

The Four Seasons!
Pets and Animal Friends!
The Age of Dinosaurs!
Baby Animals!

Homes Then and Now!
Other People, Other Homes!

Library of Congress Cataloging-in-Publication Data

Thomson, Ruth.
   The four seasons!
   (Bright idea books)
   Published in the United Kingdom under title: The seasons.
   Bibliography: p.
   Includes index.
   Summary: Describes the characteristics of the four seasons and their
effect on the plant and animal life in the park, the woods, and the meadow.
   1. Seasons—Juvenile literature. [1. Seasons]
I. Bradbury, Catherine, ill. II. Title.
QB631.T46 1985   574.5′43   85-26182
   ISBN 0-918831-64-4
   ISBN 0-918831-63-6 (lib. bdg.)

This North American edition first published in 1985 by

Gareth Stevens, Inc.
7221 West Green Tree Road   Milwaukee, Wisconsin 53223, USA

U.S. edition, this format, copyright © 1985
Supplementary text copyright © 1985 by Gareth Stevens, Inc.
Illustrations copyright © 1984 by Octopus Books Limited

First published as *The Seasons* in the United Kingdom with an original text
copyright by Octopus Books Limited.

Typeset by Ries Graphics, Ltd.
Series Editors: MaryLee Knowlton and Mark J. Sachner
Cover Design: Gary Moseley
Reading Consultant: Kathleen A. Brau

Contents

The world of nature changes with the seasons. Temperature and light vary with each season, and the plants and animals grow and change with them.

Spring in the Park

In the park in spring, trees are in bloom. The coot builds her nest of dried water plants. The mallard ducks dabble in the water. The geese eat grass beside the pond.

4

Summer in the Park

In summer, the park is full of colors. The trees have leaves and the flowers bloom brightly.

The park attendant mows the grass and tends the gardens.

All the chicks have hatched. The ducklings are born knowing how to swim! Birds hop around looking for food.

6

Autumn in the Park

In autumn, the days grow shorter and colder. The trees begin losing their leaves. The park attendant busily sweeps them off the path.

Children can find horse chestnuts and other tree fruits. Squirrels collect nuts and acorns and store them away for the winter.

Winter in the Park

In winter, the park looks very bare. Snow covers the grass, and the flower beds are empty.

The pond is frozen, so the water birds cannot find food easily. Some fly south till spring. Those that stay eagerly eat the bread children bring. Gulls and other birds fight for the crumbs.

The Woodland in Spring

After the cold, dark winter, the days grow longer. Soon the buds on the beech tree will open and leaves will grow.

The long-eared owl sleeps in a tree. Its brown feathers make it hard to spot against the tree trunk.

The fox prowls for rabbits and mice.

The wren is a shy bird. It flies from bush to bush looking for insects and caterpillars to feed its young.

A squirrel's nest is called a drey. It is made of twigs and lined with moss. Newborn squirrels sleep safely inside.

The brown creeper builds a nest behind loose bark. Its young eat beetles, woodlice, and spiders.

The male deer leaves his scent on trees and bushes. This tells other deer to stay away from his part of the woods.

Wildflowers carpet the ground. They come out early, before the leaves are on the trees.

The Woodland in Summer

Life in the Woodland in Summer

All the leaves on the trees are open now. They keep the woods cool and shady.

The baby owl sits with its mother in the tree. Its feathers will turn brown when it is a few weeks old.

A fox's home is called an earth. The cubs were born here in the spring. Now they play chasing and pouncing games. Soon they will learn to hunt.

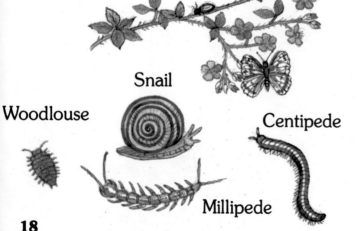

Snail

Woodlouse

Centipede

Millipede

Butterflies and beetles feed on the sweet juice, called nectar, in these bramble flowers.

Look carefully for tiny creatures like these. They usually hide among dead leaves and twigs.

18

The young squirrels follow their mother. She shows them what foods are good to eat.

The woodpecker makes a hole in a tree trunk to reach the grubs inside. It often catches insects in the air.

This deer fawn is only a few days old. It stays close to its mother. Its spotted coat helps to hide it from its enemies.

Life in the Woodland in Autumn

The weather grows colder. Most of the leaves change color and fall off. Animals and birds prepare for winter.

The nuthatch cracks a nut open with its beak and stores it in a tree.

Thrushes and jays pick ripe blackberries.

Wood mice collect berries to store over the cold winter.

Autumn is rich with mushrooms and other fungi. They grow on tree branches and fallen logs and in the rich woodland soil.

In autumn, squirrels eat acorns, beechnuts, and berries. For the winter, they hide nuts in tree hollows or in the ground.

Deer grow thicker coats. Soon they will be ready for winter.

The Woodland in Winter

Life in the Woodland in Winter

The leaves are all gone, except for the holly with its bright red berries.

The nuthatch eats insects which spend the winter in tree bark.

Snow is like a blanket. It keeps the cold air from the soil, so trees do not die.

If you look carefully, you may see tracks in the snow. These are the tracks of a fox.

The grass which the rabbits eat in summer is covered by snow. In winter, they eat bark and the shoots of young trees.

Deer gather in large groups.

They search under the snow for acorns, mosses, and shrubs. Their coats have now turned grayish-brown.

The fox digs into the snow to find mice and shrews. They burrow under the snow to keep out of the cold winds.

Squirrels stay in their drey in cold weather. They come out every few days to eat some of the food they've hidden.

The Meadow in Spring

Life in the Meadow in Spring

The animals of the meadow prepare for their babies to be born.

This male rabbit tries to impress a female. He jumps up and down and struts about on his back legs.

The field mouse lies in its nest made of dry grass. Four or five baby field mice will be born here soon. They will be warm and snug in the nest.

The queen bumblebee has been asleep all winter. Now she is building a nest in the grass, where she will lay her eggs.

Swallows come back from the warm areas where they spent the winter. They collect straw and mud to patch up their nest before they lay their eggs.

Frogs sleep all winter in holes on land. In spring, they move back to the pond to lay eggs that will become tadpoles.

Marsh marigolds are one of the first flowers to open. They grow only in damp places.

The Meadow in Summer

Life in the Meadow in Summer

Meadow flowers bloom in the summer. The grasses flower, too.

Swallows swoop low over the meadow to catch flying insects.

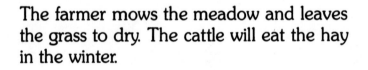

The farmer mows the meadow and leaves the grass to dry. The cattle will eat the hay in the winter.

The harvest mouse makes a nest of grass. It is shaped like a ball.

The field mouse eats grass stems.

Cattle graze in the meadow all summer long. The grass here is sweet and juicy.

Field crickets chirp in a meadow throughout the summer.

The bright colors of the flowers attract insects such as bees and butterflies. The insects feed on the nectar inside the flowers.

The Meadow in Autumn

Life in the Meadow in Autumn

The barn owl feeds mainly on field mice. It flies low over the grass at the end of the day. It listens for the field mice rustling about.

Moles dig big, deep nests for their families to live in during winter. They dig out the soil to make molehills like these.

Fewer flowers are blooming now. Buttercups, plantains, and clover are still in flower.

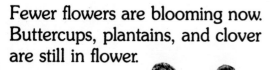

38

A flock of swallows gathers over the pond. Soon they will fly away to spend the winter in a warmer place.

The garden spider spins a big, round web. It makes a new one every day. The threads are sticky. Insects fly into the web and stick fast. The spider eats them.

The grasses and flowers have stopped growing. The farmer has stored all of the hay for the animals to eat in winter.

The Meadow in Winter

Life in the Meadow in Winter

All the flowers have died now. The trees are bare. The cattle are kept inside and eat the hay that was cut in the summer.

When it is bitterly cold by the sea, herring gulls fly inland. They feed on grubs and worms.

Foxes must travel farther than usual to find food. They search the meadow for rabbits and mice.

Flocks of geese fly high overhead. They are heading to warmer places in the South.

Crows build nests together in tall trees. Their nests are easy to spot, because the branches are bare.

The crows parade across the meadow digging for worms and grubs in the soil.

Winter will end in the park, woodland, and meadow. Spring will come again as the seasons continue in their cycle.

The following "Things to Talk About" and "Things to Do" sections, as well as the indexes of animal and plant life, offer grown-ups suggestions for further activities and ideas for young readers of *The Four Seasons!*

Things to Talk About

1. Let's look at the pictures!

    page 4: What do you think the baby is looking at?
    page 6: How many baby ducks can you find?
    pages 16-17: What kinds of baby animals do you see?

2. What animals can you name that eat food you like to eat, too?

3. Find the three different kinds of mice in the book. The Index of Animal Life can help you. How are the mice different from each other?

Things to Do

1. Choose a favorite animal to watch in the book. How do its activities change from one season to the next?

2. Look at the Index of Plant Life. What plants also grow where you live? Make a list of them and their pages. Find them in the book.

3. Look at the Index of Animal Life. Do any of these animals live where you live? Make a list of them and their page numbers. Find them in the book.

4. Make a list of the different kinds of birds you find in the book.

5. Choose a plant or animal you would like to know more about. Go to your library or bookstore and find a book that will give you more information. The list on page 47 is a good place to start looking for titles.

Index of Animal Life

Index of Plant Life

More Books About the Seasons

Here are some more books about the
seasons. If you see any books you would
like to read, see if your library or bookstore
has them.

Adventures by Leaf Light. Caldecott
  (Green Tiger Press)
Book of Seasons. Provensen (Random House)
Boy Who Didn't Believe in Spring. Clifton (Dutton)
Changing Seasons. Greydanus (Troll)
Close Looks in a Spring Woods. Welch (Dodd, Mead)
Four Stories for Four Seasons. Lionni (Pantheon)
Grandma's House. Moore (Lothrop, Lee & Shepard)
It's Snowing. Cosgrove (Dodd, Mead)
Life in the Pond. Curran (Troll)
Mouse Days: A Book of Seasons. Lionni (Pantheon)
Our Wonderful Seasons. Marcus (Troll)
Reasons for Seasons. Allison (Little, Brown)
Save the Earth: An Ecology Handbook for Kids. Miles
  (Knopf)
Seasons. (Golden Press)
Snow Fun. Levine (Watts)
Where Does the Butterfly Go When It Rains? Garelick
  (Scholastic Book Service)
Why the Sun and the Moon Live in the Sky. Dayrell
  (Houghton Mifflin)
Wonders of the Seasons. DePaola (Prentice-Hall)
Year In, Year Out. Fujikawa (Grosset & Dunlap)

For Grown-ups

The Four Seasons! is a picture book that introduces young readers to the rhythms of nature in the city, the forest, and the meadow. Simplified text and vivid two-page panoramas trace the animal and plant life of each locale through each of the four seasons. Special activities and an index of plant and animal life encourage children to develop their understanding of the cycles of the natural world through library and outdoor projects.

The editors invite interested adults to examine the sampling of reading level estimates below. Reading level estimates help adults decide what reading materials are appropriate for children at certain grade levels. These estimates are useful because they are usually based on syllable, word, and sentence counts — information that is taken from the text itself.

As useful as reading level scores are, however, we have not slavishly followed the dictates of readability formulas in our efforts to encourage young readers. Most reading specialists agree that reading skill is built on practice in reading, listening, speaking, and drawing meanings from language — activities that adults "do" when they read with children. These factors are not measured by readability scores; and yet they do enhance a text's value and appeal for children at early reading levels.

In *The Four Seasons!*, the "Contents," "Things to Talk About," "Things to Do," index, and "More Books About the Seasons" sections help children become good readers by encouraging them to use the words they read as conveyors of meaning, not as objects to be memorized. And these sections give grown-ups a chance to participate in the learning — and fun — to be found in this book.

Reading Level Analysis: FRY 3, FLESCH 89(easy), RAYGOR 5, FOG 4, SMOG 3